W9-AHW-152

# SPIES

# [WORLD WAR II] SPIES

by TIM O'SHEI

**Consultant:**
Jan Goldman, EdD
Founding Board Member
International Intelligence Ethics Association
Washington, D.C.

Capstone
Mankato, Minnesota

Edge Books are published by Capstone Press,
151 Good Counsel Drive, P.O. Box 669, Mankato, Minnesota 56002.
www.capstonepress.com

*Library of Congress Cataloging-in-Publication Data*
O'Shei, Tim.
     World War II spies / by Tim O'Shei.
     p. cm. — (Edge books. Spies)
     Summary: "Discusses the history of spying during World War II"— Provided
by publisher.
     Includes bibliographical references and index.
     ISBN-13: 978-1-4296-1307-1 (hardcover)
     ISBN-10: 1-4296-1307-6 (hardcover)
     1. World War, 1939–1945 — Secret service — Juvenile literature. 2. Espionage —
History — 20th century — Juvenile literature. I. Title. II. Title: World War Two spies.
III. Title: World War 2 spies. IV. Series.
D810.S7O74 2008
940.54'85 — dc22                                                    2007033615

**Editorial Credits**
Angie Kaelberer, editor; Bob Lentz, designer; Jo Miller, photo researcher

**Photo Credits**
AP Images, 11, 16; Gerhard Baatz, 14 (foreground); National Archives/USMC, 22
Corbis, cover (foreground); Bettmann, 21; Hulton-Deutsch Collection, 12, 13
Getty Images Inc./Express/M. McKeown, 27; Hulton Archive, 6, 18 (right);
     Roger Viollet Collection, 4; Time Life Pictures, 18 (left); Time Life Pictures/
     Andreas Feininger, 28, Bernard Hoffman, 24
Shutterstock/Aga, 1, 14 (graphic); Bas Rabeling, cover (top right); Chris Hill, cover
     (top left); Feng Yu, 5
U.S. Naval Historical Photograph, 8

1 2 3 4 5 6 13 12 11 10 09 08

# [TABLE OF CONTENTS]

. . . . . . . . . .

. . . . . . . . . .

# CHAPTER 1

# OUTSMARTING HITLER

**LEARN ABOUT:**
> Hitler's quest for power
> Double agent Garbo
> Normandy invasion

> Adolf Hitler led Germany and the Nazi party during World War II.

In the 1930s, Adolf Hitler was hungry for power. The leader of the Nazi political party in Germany wanted to take over Europe and eventually, the world.

Italy, Japan, Hungary, Romania, and Bulgaria joined Hitler in his search for power. These countries were called the Axis powers. Several countries banded together to stop them. They included Great Britain, France, and later, the United States and the Soviet Union. These countries were the Allied forces.

The result of this conflict was six years (1939–1945) of battles in Europe and Asia. But World War II was fought with more than weapons. It was also fought with intelligence. Information from spies controlled decisions on both sides.

## ARABEL'S MESSAGE

The morning of June 9, 1944, a spy code-named Arabel sent a message to Germany. Three days earlier, Allied troops had invaded the French city of Normandy.

**intelligence**

sensitive information collected or analyzed by spies

But Arabel told his Nazi bosses that the Allies invaded Normandy only to distract the Axis powers. The real action was happening in Pas de Calais, France. Based on this information, Hitler made a decision. He focused his military on protecting Calais.

Nazi officials were grateful to Arabel. The Germans thought he was one of their best spies.

>On June 6, 1944, Allied soldiers stormed the beaches of Normandy, France.

# DOUBLE AGENT

Arabel was indeed a spy, but he didn't have the Nazis' best interests at heart. Arabel was really a Spaniard named Juan Pujol. Pujol worked as a spy for Great Britain. He was a double agent who only pretended to be a German spy. His British code name was "Garbo." The British named Pujol after the actress Greta Garbo because he was also a great actor.

During World War II, Garbo fooled Germany thousands of times. He told the Nazis he had 27 spies feeding him information. None of those spies existed. Garbo also sent 400 false letters and 2,000 fake messages to Germany. The tip about Calais was an example. The Allies' real plan was to enter France through Normandy.

Garbo's trick worked. The Nazis didn't send more troops to Normandy. This fact made it easier for the Allies to retake France. That event was a major step for the Allies toward winning the war.

**double agent**

a spy who works for one country's spy agency but is really loyal to another

# CHAPTER 2

# SPIES OF THE AXIS POWERS

## LEARN ABOUT:
> Attack on Pearl Harbor
> Spies with feathers
> Axis spy rings

> The USS *Nevada* was just one of the ships damaged or destroyed during the bombing of Pearl Harbor.

Europe was a tense place during the 1930s. The economies of most countries were in bad shape. Many people had lost their jobs. The Axis powers saw the situation as an opportunity to gain power. By the late 1930s, the Axis powers were invading other countries around the world.

The United States avoided the war until December 7, 1941. That morning, Japanese airplanes attacked Pearl Harbor. This U.S. Navy base is in Hawaii. The United States declared war on Japan and joined the Allies.

Each major country had its own spy agency during the war. The Office of Strategic Services (OSS) collected intelligence for the United States. MI5 and MI6 did the same thing for Great Britain. Germany's spy agency was known as the Abwehr. The Soviet Union's spy agency was NKGB.

# SPY BIRDS

When Germany prepared to invade a country, the Nazis first set up a network of spies. These spies sent information to Germany in several ways. Some sent radio messages in Morse code. Others wrote letters using secret codes.

Spies on both sides used homing pigeons to deliver messages. In Germany, messages were tucked inside small packets fastened to the birds' legs. German travelers brought some of the birds into England. Other pigeons were dropped into England by parachute or high-speed boats. German spies in England read the messages and released the pigeons. The pigeons then flew back to their homes in Germany.

When the British learned about the "spying pigeons," they fought back. The British trained a team of larger birds called falcons to find the pigeons and kill them.

**Morse code**

a method of sending messages by radio using a series of short and long clicks

> Both the Allied forces and Axis powers used
pigeons as spy tools.

## BIG SPY RING

Germany was eager to know about U.S. goods and machines being shipped overseas. To find out, the Nazis developed a spy ring of 33 agents. The agents gathered information inside American factories and on ships.

U.S. citizen Frederick Duquesne led the spy ring. Duquesne often pretended to be a student. He wrote to American manufacturers asking for information about their factories and products. He shared news about U.S. weapons and technology with the Nazis.

William Sebold, who posed as a German spy, uncovered Duquesne's spy ring. Sebold was a double agent who worked for the Federal Bureau of Investigation (FBI). The ring was the largest ever caught as a group. The spies received prison terms ranging from 15 months to 18 years.

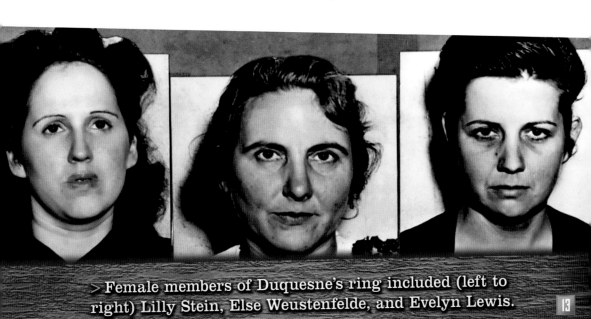

> Female members of Duquesne's ring included (left to right) Lilly Stein, Else Weustenfelde, and Evelyn Lewis.

# SPY FACT

In 1942, the U.S. government sent about
110,000 Japanese Americans to prison
camps. The government thought the
Japanese Americans might be spying
for Japan. Most of them remained in the
camps until the end of the war.

## SPIES ON THE SHORE

Germany also wanted to disrupt U.S. manufacturing and frighten the American people. In June 1942, two German submarines crept beneath the water to the U.S. coast. One sub came to shore at Ponte Vedra Beach in Florida. The other surfaced near Long Island, New York. Each sub held four Germans who were disguised as Americans. They spoke English and understood American culture. They were trained to attack weapons factories.

Though the Germans sneaked into the United States successfully, one of them became scared of being caught. Six days after arriving, George Dasch turned himself in to the FBI. Dasch helped the FBI find the others. All eight were arrested, and six of them were put to death. Dasch was one of the two whose lives were spared.

# CHAPTER 3

# THE ALLIES STRIKE BACK

## LEARN ABOUT:
> A newspaper spy
> Britain's Double-Cross
> Decoding Enigma

> Richard Sorge helped keep
Moscow from falling to the Nazis.

While the Axis powers planted spies in Allied nations, the Allies were doing the same thing in Axis countries.

Richard Sorge was a reporter for a German newspaper in Tokyo, Japan. Or so it seemed. Sorge was actually a Soviet spy. His most important tip helped stop the Nazis from taking control of the Soviet capital, Moscow.

In 1941, the Soviet military prepared to defend itself against both Germany and Japan. Thousands of Soviet soldiers were in Siberia to protect the central and western Soviet Union.

Sorge learned that Japan planned to overtake southeast Asia. That meant the Soviets didn't need to worry about the Japanese. But Soviet leader Joseph Stalin still needed to protect his most important city. Stalin sent troops from Siberia to Moscow to help hold off the Nazis.

Soon after Sorge sent that information, the Japanese caught him and put him in jail. They killed him three years later.

# SPY FILES: CRACKING THE CODE MACHINE

In 1933, three Polish mathematicians completed a tough task. They figured out how to read messages coded by Germany's Enigma machine. The word "enigma" means "mystery." The machine used a keyboard and spinning disks to create complex codes that hid secret messages.

Once they broke the code, the mathematicians were able to make copies of the machine. In July 1939, Poland gave Enigma copies to Great Britain and France. These countries used the machines to read secret Nazi messages.

When Germany invaded Poland in September 1939, the three mathematicians fled to France. There, they worked as message decoders for the Allies.

# DOUBLE-CROSS SYSTEM

In war, leaders face difficult decisions. Intelligence from spies helps them make smart choices.

Of course, that strategy works only when the information is true. Many World War II spies spread false information. They hoped to trick enemies into making bad decisions.

The British spy agency MI5 built a large network of double agents. MI5 broke a code used by the Abwehr. The British then decoded a long list of German spies working in Britain. They captured as many German spies as possible and made them an offer. They could spy for the Allies or be put to death. This plan was called the "Double-Cross" system.

Britain had about 120 double-cross agents. They specialized in disinformation. The agents gave information to their German contacts, just as they always had. But now, that information was mostly false. It helped convince Germany that the Allied military was mightier than it actually was.

# SPY FILES: HINTS OF AN ATTACK

Clues from a spy can help prevent major attacks. Sometimes, though, those clues are overlooked.

In 1941, the Nazis sent Dusan "Dusko" Popov to the United States. Popov was actually a double agent whose real loyalty was to the Allies.

The Nazis asked Popov to find out information about the U.S. Navy base at Pearl Harbor, Hawaii. Popov told the FBI about the Nazis' request, but FBI Director J. Edgar Hoover wasn't concerned. He should have been, though. On December 7, 1941, Japanese bombers killed about 2,400 people at Pearl Harbor.

That information made the Nazis more cautious. They were less aggressive against the Allies than they might have been. Eventually, the Allies got the upper hand. In that way, spies were important to the outcome of the war.

# CHAPTER 4

# VICTORY!

## LEARN ABOUT:

> Navajo code talkers
> Axis surrender
> Aftermath of World War II

> Navajo code talkers sent messages that the Japanese couldn't decode.

After the Allies' success invading Normandy, it was clear that the Axis powers were losing the war in Europe. On April 28, 1945, Italian leader Benito Mussolini was killed by his own people. Two days later, Hitler killed himself as the Allies closed in on him.

On May 8, Germany surrendered to the Allies. The Allies then turned all of their attention to fighting Japan.

## OUTSMARTING JAPAN

The Japanese were skilled at decoding Allied messages. But there was one code they could never crack.

The language of the Navajo American Indians is complicated. For many years, the language had no written alphabet. For these reasons, the Navajo language is difficult for outsiders to learn. The U.S. Marines recruited about 400 Navajos called code talkers. Their job was to translate secret English messages into Navajo. The code talkers then sent the messages by radio or telephone.

**Navajo**

an American Indian group from the western United States

移轉先
立山町八五三番地
北部第五組　田川横方
深堀蓼雄

> Japanese cities were destroyed by the U.S. bombs.

The Navajos worked quickly. They could decode and send a three-line English message in as little as 20 seconds.

During the Battle of Iwo Jima in 1945, six Navajo code talkers worked for 48 hours. They sent about 800 messages and made no mistakes. The Allies defeated the Japanese at that battle and the Battle of Okinawa that followed.

But the Japanese still refused to surrender. In August 1945, the United States exploded two atomic bombs in Japan. The destruction was huge. Japan officially surrendered September 2. The war was finally over.

## SPY FACT

The U.S. atomic bombs fell on the Japanese cities of Hiroshima and Nagasaki. At least 70,000 people were killed in Hiroshima and 40,000 in Nagasaki. Many others died later from radiation sickness.

## WAR'S AFTERMATH

Wars don't have happy endings, though, even for the winners. Much of Europe and parts of Asia were destroyed. The Allies needed to rebuild those countries.

But the United States and the Soviet Union disagreed on several major points. Over the next few years, the relationship between the two countries worsened. This started a new era in history — and spying — called the Cold War.

## SPY FACT

During the war, famous entertainer Josephine Baker spied for France. She carried messages written in invisible ink on her sheet music.

# SPY FILES: THE REAL BOND

Ever wonder how the fictional spy James Bond became so popular? The author who created him was a spy in real life.

Ian Fleming wrote the James Bond books on which the modern-day movies were based. Fleming grew up in Great Britain. He worked as a spy for the British Navy during World War II. Many of the daring and creative missions Fleming planned were too risky for the British government to attempt. But later, Fleming had James Bond perform some of these clever missions in his books.

> After Germany's surrender on May 8, 1945, Americans gathered in Times Square in New York City.

## SPYING GETS RESULTS

Spies don't win wars alone, but they surely help. Richard Sorge helped the Soviet Union defend its most important city. Britain's Double-Cross system confused the Germans. The spy Garbo tricked Hitler into not focusing on the Normandy invasion.

The Allies won World War II with soldiers and weapons. But they needed a plan for how and when to use their military power. Their plan was strengthened by secret information that could only come from spies.

# GLOSSARY

**atomic bomb** (uh-TAH-mik BOM) — a powerful explosive that destroys large areas

**culture** (KUHL-chuhr) — the way of life, customs, ideas, and traditions of a group of people

**disinformation** (dis-in-for-MAY-shuhn) — false information spread on purpose

**double agent** (DUH-buhl AY-juhnt) — a spy who works for one country's spy agency but is really loyal to another

**Enigma** (uh-NIG-muh) — Germany's coding machine

**intelligence** (in-TEH-luh-juhnss) — sensitive information collected or analyzed by spies

**Morse code** (MORSS KODE) — a method of sending messages by radio using a series of long and short clicks

**Navajo** (NAH-vuh-hoe) — an American Indian group from the western United States

**Nazi Party** (NOT-see PAR-tee) — the German political party led by Adolf Hitler; the name was short for National Socialist German Workers' Party.

# READ MORE

**Buranelli, Vincent.** *American Spies and Traitors.* Collective Biographies. Berkeley Heights, N.J.: Enslow, 2004.

**Coleman, Janet Wyman.** *Secrets, Lies, Gizmos, and Spies: A History of Spies and Espionage.* New York: Harry N. Abrams, 2006.

**Dowswell, Paul, and Fergus Fleming.** *True Spy Stories.* True Adventure Stories. London: Usborne Books, 2004.

**Walker, Kate, and Elaine Argaet.** *Super Spies of World War II.* Spies and Spying. North Mankato, Minn.: Smart Apple Media, 2003.

# INTERNET SITES

FactHound offers a safe, fun way to find Internet sites related to this book. All of the sites on FactHound have been researched by our staff.

Here's how:
1. Visit *www.facthound.com*
2. Choose your grade level.
3. Type in this book ID **1429613076** for age-appropriate sites. You may also browse subjects by clicking on letters, or by clicking on pictures and words.
4. Click on the **Fetch It** button.

**FactHound will fetch the best sites for you!**

# INDEX